RED

FLAGS

NEGATIVE SIGNS=

He Is NOT The One!

IO112233

AUDREA V. HEARD

© 2021
IBG Publications, Inc.
www.ibgpublications.com

AUDREA V. HEARD

Published by I.B.G. Publications, Inc., a Power to Wealth Company

Web Address: WWW.IBGPublications.Com

admin@IBGPublications.Com / 904-419-9810

Copyright, 2022 by Audrea V. Abraham

IBG Publications, Inc., Orange Park, FL

ISBN: 978-1-956266-65-8

Heard, Audrea V.

Red Flags: Negative Signs He Is Not The One

Printed in the United States of America.

DEDICATION

This book is dedicated to Single Women

Dating and finding a mate is not easy. But what IS easy? Listening to the voice of God and heeding the RED FLAGS!

To my ex-husband. You taught me the Red Flags, and for that, I am eternally grateful. I am grateful because I will NEVER marry another man whose RED FLAGS are not unaddressed.

Thanks dear.

AUDREA V. HEARD

TABLE OF CONTENTS

AUDREA V. HEARD

ACKNOWLEDGMENTS

I acknowledge my Father, God, who is my
continual inspiration for every book I write.

You allow me to have experience to teach and train
others. This book is no exception. Remain with me
and guide me as I help women to heal from the
wounds experienced while attempting
to find true love.

I acknowledge my sister/confidante, *Tamora
Johnson*. You have been an amazing, listening ear
while I navigated my course in finding true love.
You have not judged me but applauded me when I
sought out my truth and found it.
I love you sis!!

AUDREA V. HEARD

INTRODUCTION

Ding!!

There went my Facebook Messenger alert.

Surprised, it was a message from an old friend. Unaware of his motives or intentions, I answered with joy, happy to hear from him. It was the following conversation that stole seven years from my life. 😩

Let me explain…

He went on to tell me how he missed me, appreciated the times I prayed for him and how he wished he would have had the opportunity to spend more time with me.

After a few more exchanges of conversations, he would go on to tell me how he "believed" I was his wife.

Belief.

9

Who was he *believing* told him this? His instincts? His idea of preying on an unexpected victim? Perhaps it was him comparing the version of me he had separated from some years prior.

Until this day, I am still not sure how he came to the conclusion that I was his wife. But what I AM sure of? He did NOT hear God. Nope, he did not.

A Love Affair Moving Too Fast...

After having several conversations with him about me being his wife, somehow, he "convinced" me that I was, "the one."

I say, "He convinced me," because GOD never said I was his wife. What God distinctly told me is that he loved me, but not the latter. I mixed up love for a green light.

Someone loving you can actually be a, "red flag," because that love can be toxic, filled with ill motives and intentions. When someone tells you they, "love you," especially right away, you must question the motive and agenda behind that love.

It was around about March when I was proposed to by telephone: **RED FLAG!** Later that month in March, he was on a train ride to visit me with a ticket that **I** paid for: **RED FLAG!** And when he arrived, he did not even have the ring, NOR did he get down on one knee to officially propose to me. **ALL RED FLAGS!!**

I see this book will host **MANY** Red Flags, lol.

It was *more* than a Red Flag when he came to visit and refused to return to where he came from. This was all in the name of, "I cannot live without you." The Red Flags were beyond evident, but I was captured in the euphoria of: *He Loves me*.

Everything moved too fast. Not to mention that we set the original date of our wedding for that coming October. He thought a Fall wedding would be romantic, yet we rushed into marriage early May; not revealing to anyone we were already married.

The crazy thing is that to this day, I really do not remember what date we got married. It was particularly between May 1st through the 3rd.

My memory refuses to recollect the date.

***

Here are some things I neglected to do during my stage of euphoria:

- ✓ Perform a credit check.
- ✓ Check for stable, consistent, reliable income.

✓ Run a criminal history check.
✓ Ask for his history of paying bills.
✓ Command a real marriage proposal.
✓ *Require* he gain employment when he moved in.
✓ Check out his relationship with God.
✓ Go deeper with God for answers.
✓ Understand his role in my *future*.
✓ Heed the Red Flags.
✓ Heed the warnings from my family (who identified his trickery).
✓ Ensure he had cast out his life demons and gained true deliverance.

These were all things I neglected to do before saying, "I do." I was just happy someone wanted to actually marry me, regardless of their status.

When you have never been married, and have no children, it is no easy task to do your due diligence when you are craving for love. I was craving for love yet did not love myself enough to wait on the man God had for my life. I wanted to get it done, (marriage) and I was in love with this crazy notion that my husband would just, *know* when he met me.

Somewhere between that fantasy of the, "knowing," and being told so quickly, I believed the lie and accepted this counterfeit relationship.

It all just moved too fast. 😵

Why did I write this book??

I wrote this book because of the recent events of men coming in and out of my life with this same agenda. They too were filled with these same words, "You are my wife."

If I had about $100 for every time I was told this, I'd probably be banking up on $10K or so. That is probably an exaggeration, but I am sure I have heard this lie at least 5-6 times in the last five years or so.

Initially, it was challenging to refute this statement. When I made "The Vow," it became easier to demand more information about this statement from the person giving it.

The enemy was sending men who were packaged right on both ends of the spectrum. He sent the "type" of man I liked who were from the region I believe to marry a man from.

This made it more challenging because I thought I was attracting the love I deserved. That's why I made, "The Vow," right?

Yes.

But what was I *not* doing? Continuing to exercise my discernment, the Red Flags were hitting me left and right.

I extend gratitude to God because He did not allow me to get back into the same love trap. The Red Flags this time around became hot and heavy.

In one relationship, I was manipulated with a Red Flag. The second time around, the Red Flags were so obvious that I would be sheep to the slaughter if I did not heed the warnings.

It is always my hope to reach someone through the tests and trials of my life. I aim to do as the Bible instructs me to do-when you are converted, strengthen thy brother. In this case, I plan to strengthen my *sisters*.

This book title came up between a conversation amongst a sister/friend and me. I plan to write a book titled, 'Green Flags: Positive Signs He IS the One! In the sequel, we will talk about the Green Flags, and it will be a more pleasant journey for our sisters.

But for the time being, this is about my personal healing, and I have to exercise that healing by writing this book about my own personal journey in dealing with these Red Flags.

It was during an exchange with one of these recent men claiming me as wife that the need for healing was triggered.

What was this trigger?

They asked me for money, way too soon. I am talking about a week into this relationship. This "favor" was asked all in the name of me being their "wife" in name only. The authentic truth is this was just an online connection up until the point of them asking for this favor.

What happened when they asked? I totally shut down, froze up, and could hardly speak. What I did not realize at that moment was there was healing that still needed to take place from the wounds my ex-husband had inflicted.

The truth of the matter is that I had masked the pain. Moved past it, but not dealt with it. I did not lay on the operating table so the Holy Spirit could cut the pain out of my heart.

Why did this pain need to be cut out? Because I will marry again, and my 'real' husband may just ask me for money. And his request may be a valid, needed request. I can't freeze up on the man God truly has

15

sent my way when he may have a financial need that I am able to assist him with.

The, "I have been burnt" syndrome had risen up in me, and I was now sitting there needing to deal with this pain. Not because the person who was asking for the money caused the pain, but because the person who truly caused the pain was running around free to burn someone else. But yet, I was sitting there in that prison of pain.

No, Audrea won't stay there, she just won't. I went to the threshing floor. For those who are not familiar with the "Threshing Floor," it is a place of prayer and pruning. A place where God can truly heal you and deliver you from whatever is ailing you.

And you know what? The NEXT time I was asked for money, from this same person, I did not feel that pain again. Why? Because I knew that the gig on this person was up, they were out to use and abuse me. And I was NOT having that again.

The same morning they asked for the money, I had to hear from God. I wanted to know if this person was an imposter and if I really was their wife. I could not refute the possibility, and honestly, I really wanted to be their wife. They had such great potential (another Red Flag when not matched to your potential).

So, I went out on my daily walk because my spirit was troubled by their request. HOW are they asking me for money TWO weeks into this relationship? HOW are they requesting me to go against one of my number one rules?

What is that rule?

A man should not be asking a woman for money. This rule is not etched in stone anywhere, nor is it a "relationship rule." It is a rule I desire to live by because it seems to give me some sort of safety from being used and abused.

Why?

Because any man who means you good, will find his own means for making money and making his ends meet up. That is **IF** he means you good.

When he does not, he will find every way to make a come up off of your back, resources and income. He is not looking for his own means because he is interested in what *you* worked hard to achieve.

Ladies, we are going for a ride, and I pray you have your seat belt on. If not, buckle up, you are going for the ride of your life. But it will be a good ride because it will bring healing to areas of your life that the Father desires you to no longer be blind, or burned to your core.

He loves you, and so do I.

Let's take this ride!

CHAPTER i:

EUPHORIA OR TRUE LOVE?

EUPHORIA

Euphoria is defined by the Merriam-Webster Dictionary as a feeling of wellbeing or elation.

With this definition, what on earth could be wrong with wanting to be in a state of euphoria?

Well, the danger in being in a constant state of euphoria means that you may never be in a position to make right or sound decisions. Never having a sober mind means there is no balance to your relationship, placing you in a danger zone.

Experiencing euphoria can be likened to being high off of some sort of drug. This is because the hormone dopamine is released into the blood stream and is

19

considered a part of the body's reward system. It is associated with a pleasurable sensation along with memory, learning, and other bodily functions.

A *constant* reward is not always a good thing.

Everyone wants to always be happy, but that is not our reality. The truth is pain and suffering are as much a part of our life as happiness is. But when there is no balance, and you are always floating around, there is bound to be something hiding out and lurking underneath the shadows.

I floated in euphoria for about the first 12 months of my first marriage. Always happy, always eating, and always in the dark about my reality.

So… What was really going on Audrea?

My account was always in the negative and bills were coming in left and right. Checks were bouncing like a basketball rolling down a never-ending court of euphoria and bliss, and I couldn't stop the dribble. I was in such denial about the wreck that happened to my life for floating around ignoring the signs that were screaming out at me all for the sake of, "love."

It was well into the second year of the marriage when the blinders were ripped from my eyes. The exposure to the light of, "truth," gave way to a bright, piercing light of agony and pain.

I did *not* hear God to marry this man. I heard my flesh and self-will. Not the will of God. I was deep into a marriage with someone who was struggling with their sexuality, and they were using me not only as a "beard," but I was providing him with a safe and secure home to live in. Not to mention he was well taken care of, with *my* salary, credit, and integrity.

You see, my integrity was the main commodity on the line in this marriage. If you are someone who has never worked to build your integrity, then you have no idea what it means when someone comes along and snatches the house you built down.

But if you have worked to build your reputation and the trust of people, God's people, then you are well aware of what it means to have your integrity house come tumbling down.

This man not only stole my integrity, but he also tarnished my criminal record: something I did not possess up until that point. You see, prior to the fateful day I married him in May of 2010, I did not possess a criminal record. I did not know what jail was like, and I had not spent any time in a jail outside of a visit to a former boyfriend. Prison and jail did not know my name.

I was not aware of court processes or what it meant if you could not afford an attorney. All I knew is that I was having my fingerprints taken, frowning for a mug shot, and spending the night in jail, sleeping on a very thin mat on a cement floor.

This was _not_ a place fitting for a queen.

Due to the fact that this was my first and only offense, the judge seemed to have mercy on me. He instructed me to pay the court fees and costs and go home. He was quite perplexed that I was arrested and held on for such a petty crime.

But how, oh how was I able to be released from that jail cell, and return with a happy heart to a man who had caused me to end up there in the first place? How was I happy to embrace the enemy of my destiny? How was I walking out of that court happy that he used _my_ money to bail me out? He did not even have a bank account with money in it to get me out of jail.

I was happy to see him because I was in a state of euphoria, which caused me to go blind to the train wreck my life had become. If this was not a sign that God was not in this marriage, I do not know what was. The marriage was not even 60 days old and I should have taken off running for dear life.

But instead, I was trapped in a state of…..

EUPHORIA.

Do I regret this decision? Absolutely. It stole about seven years from my life, although the marriage only lasted about four years on paper, two years of actually being together. All for the sake of, "love."

Love will lend you heartache and the only remedy is to exit stage left. It was not until I embraced the bright light that I was able to break this soul tie which developed from a broken place in my life.

I expound on my brokenness in my book, *Peace in Broken Places: Exposing Lies & Toxic Ties*. This relationship was a direct result of the death of my mother, along with many others. Once I got to the root of the development of this toxic tie, I was able to move beyond my state of euphoria. This was when I began dealing with the reality of what my life had become.

The Breakup…

Divorce was inevitable. I filed the papers and broke a tie that was not an easy one to break. But nevertheless, I took that tall glass of water and swallowed that bitter pill: I missed God.

I had made such a fiasco of what it meant to, "hear God." I had put God's name on this marriage, and He was no where in sight. Well, He was in sight, I was just ignoring His presence in the room. I ignored His soft and gentle nudges when He was showing me the signs that a mistake was on the horizon.

And yet, instead of taking off running, and annulling the marriage (which no one was really aware had occurred), I continued on in this parade of a marriage, all in the name of, *'love,'* 'I heard God,' and all the other shenanigans that cause us to move too fast.

So….. Let's Talk about love.

LOVE

The Merriam Webster Dictionary defines Love as:
-Strong affection for another arising out of kinship or personal ties.
-Attraction based on sexual desire: affection and tenderness felt by lovers.
-Affection based on admiration, benevolence, or common interests.

After learning more about love and what it truly means, what have been some of the reasons that you have fallen in love with a man? What has been kinship or personal tie? Has it been sexual desires, some sort of admiration, or were you given gifts which caused you to fall…….in love?

We hear this word love, and for so many people, it can bear a different meaning. We also know there are various types of love, and there are *The Five Love Languages*®, penned by Author Gary Chapman.

But my question is, what does love mean to you?

I am going to take a very brief look at the different types of love so you can determine the basis upon which to build your male-based relationships. These love types also play a role as to where to compartmentalize the men in your life.

My ex-husband started in my life in the realm of, "friendship," or what is best known as, "Philia" love. This is where our love should have remained. But we crossed the realm into erotic love, which was the beginning of our failure and the end of our friendship.

Upon some research, I ran across a website which listed eight different types of love.

(**www.ftd.com/blog/give/types-of-love**)

Up until this point, I was probably only aware of about maybe four different types of love, so it was refreshing to learn more about love types. Especially since most of my readers have most likely been exposed to the types of love I will discuss from this site.

Here are the 8 different types of love:

1) **Philia**: Affectionate Love
   -A love that runs deep in true friendships.
   Love catalyst: Mind.
   -*Ways to show this love*: exchange your beliefs and imperfections with close friends.
   Philia is love without romantic attraction and occurs between friends or family members. It occurs when both people share the same values and respect each other. It is commonly referred to as, "brotherly love."

2) **Pragma**: Enduring Love
   -Mature love that develops over time.
   Love catalyst: Subconscious.
   Ways to show this love: put effort into long-term and reciprocated relationships.
   Pragma is a unique bonded love that matures over many years. It's an everlasting love between a couple that chooses to put equal

effort into their relationship. Commitment and dedication are required to reach, "Pragma." Instead of, "falling in love," you are, "standing in love" with the partner you want by your side indefinitely.

3) **Storge:** Familiar Love
-Flows between parents and children or childhood friends.
Love catalyst: Memories.
***Ways to show this love*:** Show gratitude towards the people close to you.
Storge is a naturally occurring love rooted in parents and children, as well as best friends. It is an infinite love built upon acceptance and deep emotional connection. This love comes easily and immediately in parent and child relationships.

4) **Eros:** Romantic Love
-Personal infatuation and physical pleasure.
Love Catalyst: Body.
***Ways to show this love*:** Engage in physical touch such as hugging or kissing.
Eros is a primal love that comes as a natural instinct for most people. It's a passionate love displayed through physical affection. These romantic behaviors include, but are not limited to, kissing, hugging and holding

27

hands. This love is a desire for another person's physical body.

5) **Ludas:** Playful Love
-Flirting and beginning stages of intimate love.
Love Catalyst: Emotion.
Ways to show this love: Express a flirtatious interest in who you admire.
Ludas is a child-like and flirtatious love commonly found in the beginning stages of a relationship (AKA the honeymoon stage). This type of love consists of teasing, playful motives and laughter between two people. Although common in young couples, older couples who strive for this love find a more rewarding relationship.

6) **Mania:** Obsessive Love
-Obsessiveness or madness over a love partner.
Love Catalyst: Survival.
How to avoid this love: Focus on yourself more verses another person.
Mania is an obsessive love towards a partner. It leads to unwanted jealousy or possessiveness-known as co-dependency. Most cases of obsessive love are found in couples with an imbalance of love towards each other. An imbalance of *Eros* and *Ludas*

is the main cause of *Mania*. With healthy levels of playful and romantic love, this harmful and obsessive love can be avoided.

7) **Philautia**: Self Love
-Having a healthy, "self-compassion" love towards oneself.
Love Catalyst: Soul.
Ways to show this love: Respect, accept and appreciate yourself.
Philautia is a healthy form of love where you recognize your self-worth and don't ignore your personal needs. Self-love begins with acknowledging your responsibility for your well-being. It's challenging to exemplify the outbound types of love because you can't offer what you don't have.

8) **Agape:** Selfless Love
-An empathetic attitude of love for everyone and anyone.
Love Catalyst: Spirit.
*Ways to show this love***:** Express unconditional love in any situation.
Agape is the highest level to offer love. It's given without any expectations of receiving anything in return. Offering Agape is a decision to spread love in any circumstances- including destructive situations. Agape is not

29

a physical act, it's a feeling, but acts of self-love can elicit Agape since self-monitoring leads to results.

Now that we have looked at the different forms of love, I want you to evaluate past and current relationships. Determine what type of love existed between the two of you and when it transitioned into eros love. Did it start with eros, yet no other love had the opportunity to exist?

These are honest conversations that you should have with yourself so that you can come to terms with what went wrong, and when. A relationship not balanced will lead to Red Flags waving and ending with broken promises and dead dreams.

Here is a quick question hit list I want you to ask yourself about your past and present relationships:

- ✓ How did the love affair start?
- ✓ What type of love existed between he and I?
- ✓ What was good about our love? Where did our love go wrong?
- ✓ Are we able to shift gears in our love so that we can preserve this relationship? Will love actually preserve this relationship, or do we need to build on something else?

Believe it or not, we do not really look at what type of love existed in our male relationships. This is because most times we based our male love-based relationships on *eros* love. This is because we believe it should start with a physical attraction or it won't go anywhere. But we fail to realize that *pragma* love will carry the relationship and give it longevity.

Ask yourself this question, "Was our love balanced, or was it based solely on euphoria? Did we float around in euphoria for years, and then reality hit us in the face when traumatic events occurred?"

You see, trauma to individuals in a relationship or both individuals collectively will show you exactly what type of love exists. Is your, "love" able to weather through these life storms, or is it crumbling under the pressure? These are some things to consider when we express this thing called, love and decide if we will spend the remainder of our lives with someone.

If euphoria kept you in a place where you were not able to explore the type of love that existed between you and the man in your life, then you must go back and revisit when it began and where it went wrong. Most times, euphoria is mistaken as love, yet mixed in with *eros*, without a foundation established in *agape*. Then hardships come, and the relationship is not built on anything solid enough to hold it together.

Explore your relationship love points. Make the proper plan moving forward to ensure that your love is built on the type of love that builds relationships. Euphoria fades and dissipates; it does *not* hold two individuals together.

Check your love life!

CHAPTER 2:

NARCISSISTIC BEHAVIORS

NARCISSIST

Narcissist is defined by the Merriam-Webster Dictionary as an individual showing symptoms of or suffering from narcissism such as an extremely self-centered person who has an exaggerated sense of self-importance.

My dealings with a narcissistic man were short, yet interesting. The thing about getting your spirit right before God and purging from bad male relationships is that it heightens your discernment. Things become exposed that you may not be clear on, yet, you know something is not right.

I have to tell this story because it brought my deliverance and truly showed me who God was *not*.

He was *not* manifesting Himself through this person as my husband. This person was self-centered and walking in their own measure of grace and *not* the grace of God. They were extending their own grace, which ran short when their controlling tactics were no longer working on me.

But guess what ladies? Somehow, the way he infiltrated my life impressed me and turned me on in some sort of weird way. I liked his way of being forward, and his boldness did something strange for my ego. I liked what he said to me, although it was an extremely off way to approach a woman.

The beginning of his conversation was, "I prayed about you, the Lord told me you are my wife, and that you are my property. I have come to claim my property."

Your *property*?

Uhm, excuse me sir, I am no one's property besides the Lord. Even in a covenant marriage relationship, we *still* belong to God. We do not become the, 'property' of our spouse, because ultimately, we belong to God.

To all of my religious zealots, please do not come for me with the scripture in *I Corinthians 7:4*. This scripture is explicitly speaking in the sense of sexual experiences between husband and wife. This scripture shows us how there should be mutual consent in how sexual relations should be handled in the sense of abstinence. This scripture is not relevant to how I was approached by this, "spirit husband."

When I talk about *not* being your spouse's property, I mean it in the sense of property as in a car, house, clothes, shoes, etc. This is how he approached me.

When someone believes that you are their **property**, this means that they believe they can tell you when to come, and when to go. They can use you as a profitable piece of machinery in order to make them money. Now you become *their* resource and they depend more on you than God. When you are their *property*, it means what they say goes, and you have no opinion. And if you voice your opinion, they are quick to tell you that you are wrong or not in submission to *their* authority.

This is the mind and thought process of a Narcissist.

They are all about their own personal gain, and what the relationship can produce for *them*. This person came across as self-important and did not even consider how I felt about his claim to me. He assumed the earth revolved around him, he was the sun, and no one around him was worthy enough to be the moon. I did not refute his claims because remember I said that it fed my ego in some sort of strange way?

The enemy is so cunning and conniving. He comes in ways that can sneak up on us because he has been studying us since the day we were born. He knows what pleases our flesh, what tantalizes our senses, and what gives our egos the boost needed in order to keep us in the, "love" trap.

I was entertaining some sort of twisted thinking that when a man was forward with me, this is what I needed. I convinced myself, I am a strong woman, and I need a man who is not passive, but can control me when I get out of line.

Thinking this way attracted a man to me who decided he would take rule over me and make me his, 'property.' I had not come to the realization that the man in my life is not designed to control me. There has to be a balance between leading, taking the lead, yet not overriding my free will.

Believe it or not, this was an engagement and love affair that did not make it for 90 days. After dealing with him, I became clear about what type of man I needed and what my assignment is as a wife. No man should be in control of me, and I am no man's property.

Remember when I said that I got delivered from certain behaviors of men? This means that your deliverance can be real, but yet the enemy can send someone who sneaks up on you, bangs you across the head and now you are seeing stars. Yet when the stars fade, you begin to realize that it is *not* the will of God to be controlled, forced to fulfill someone else's will and desires, walking in total obedience to *their* belief system.

As I look back on my dealings with this narcissist, I realize that when I stopped listening to him and **everything** he told me to do, he realized that he could not exert his will over me. His time was running out QUICKLY! The narcissistic behaviors manifested to the point where he told me I was not hearing God because I would not obey what he was telling me to do.

This was a major Red Flag!

When someone tries to make you believe that they are the *only* way to get to God, hear God, and have what God has for you: this person is narcissistic and desires to be worshipped above God. Watch out and take heed ladies, this is *not* a person to be yoked up with and in covenant with. It will *always* be about *them*, and you will become a shadow in the background as they shine like the sun.

I took the time to do some research to locate the signs of narcissistic behaviors. This will help you identify what you are dealing with, and how to handle this personality type moving forward.

According to **Healthline.com**, these are the 9 official criteria for narcissistic personality disorder:

➢ Grandiose sense of self-importance.
➢ Preoccupation with fantasies of unlimited success, power, brilliance, beauty or ideal love.
➢ Belief they're special and unique and can only be understood by, or should associate with, other special or high-status people or institutions.
➢ Need for excessive admiration.
➢ Sense of entitlement.
➢ Interpersonally exploitative behavior.
➢ Lack of empathy.
➢ Envy of others or a belief that others are envious of them.
➢ Demonstration of arrogant and haughty behaviors or attitudes.

When I look at these criteria, it resonates so much with my experience with this person. I can recall an incident where he approached someone very dear to me, telling *them* how self-centered *they* were. The person he approached did not respond to his phone call in the time frame he desired, so he considered them, "arrogant." He outright called them arrogant, and everything else that goes along with this territory.

Sir, how ridiculously self-centered can you be? How much importance should we bestow upon *you*, your highness?

Then there was the time that we were, "working together," and he wanted me to change something on the business website that was absolutely, grammatically incorrect! When I did not, "correct" it based on what *he* said, he became angry and accused me of being rebellious and not submitting to his authority. I had to prove to him that what he said was wrong, and show him his error. Still not receptive to what I had to say, he goes on to tell me that I approached him wrong, and I was not soft enough in correcting him. When someone does not want to be wrong, no matter what or *how* you say it, it will *always* be something wrong in your approach.

Let's not even discuss the fact that this business that we were working, "together," I had taken on *all* the expenses of getting it up and running. I was the one paying for the website, logo, email address, and every other expense that came along with getting this venture going.

Take note here ladies: If you start a business venture with a man, and he does not contribute anything but intellectual property, you need to make sure it is in writing how this business will run and how profits will be divided up. If things are not in writing, *or* recorded on video/audio, you have nothing to reference how the business will run. If it comes down to a battle in court with a business that becomes very profitable, you could walk away taking a major hit.

In this business, I brought the bulk of the business to the table. He contributed, but ultimately, I was the *main* contributor, and it was *my* vision. Everything he was able to bring to the table, I had to put in the blood, sweat and tears to bring it to life. Not to mention that as a woman, I provided my womb, which gave him the power of reproduction and multiplication.

As women, we *are* the ones who, incubate and birth the vision to life. A man plants a seed, but we are the incubators who nourish that seed and produce a baby.

Remember the *power* of your womb, whether natural or spiritual.

The problem in this situation is that I gave him more authority than he deserved. I made him a co-founder, when *I* was the founder of this particular business approximately six years *prior* to him coming onto the, "team." He had not invested enough time *or* intellectual property to maintain that role. He was given too much, too soon, and too quickly. I regretted it all shortly after I decided to end the relationship because his narcissistic ways began to rear their ugly head.

It All Came Crashing Down...

I called a Zoom meeting (which was recorded) to advise him that the relationship was ending along with the partnership. After I completed everything I desired to say, which was really too little too late, the demon in him manifested and went off on me across that video like I had never seen him behave before. As I sit here and ponder on what he said and his response to me, if we were in the same room, I am sure he would have pounced on me.

The problem here is that God never released me to be with this man. I prayed, but God *never* said he was the one. I was convinced because of who he was, and the region he originated from, all because of the *type*

41

of man the Lord told me I would marry. These factors influenced me, causing me to say, "yes" to something that would have put me outside of the will of God for my life. He imposed *his* influence over me, causing me to accept his proposal. There is a huge difference.

All of this was coupled together with his grandiose ideas that he fed me about doing ministry together and how great of a couple we would become for the, "kingdom" of God. He made promises of how many churches we would plant, and the people whom would follow us. He would go as far as to compare us to other notable couples who did ministry together and how their start was similar to ours, and the *potential* we had to be great.

Notice I said, "***potential***."

Potential not manifested can be a dangerous thing when the *hope* of the potential is to be built on your back. Read that again ladies and ponder on it for a while.

As of late, I have come to realize that the man I will marry will not be a man whom I will do ministry within the traditional sense of it. Marriage *is* ministry but what type of ministry are he and I supposed to do, 'together?' This is something that we as ladies should be thinking about when we enter into covenant.

The church has convinced us that we should be doing ministry a particular type of way, based on the "perception" of team/marriage ministry. But God has a unique and detailed path for those whom *He* has ordained to be together. This is the calling we should seek but can only be found when we have identified our own unique purpose. When we join up with a man, he has to be walking in his own, "purpose."

Looking at the narcissistic personality and how it operates has opened my eyes and enlightened me on so many levels. It is my hope and prayer that it has done the same for you, and you won't be entangled by this yoke of bondage.

"If you ignore the red flags, embrace the heartache to come."

— *Amanda Mosher*

CHAPTER 3:

THE WOMAN OR THE FANTASY?

FANTASY

Fantasy is defined by the Merriam-Webster Dictionary as the power or process of creating especially unrealistic or improbable mental images in response to psychological need.

Before we talk about the fantasy, let's first talk about the psychological needs that men have. If I am to be more specific, let's deal with the needs that men have based on my own experiences.

Now, allow me to insert this caveat: I have not done any extensive research on men, their wants, desires or psychological needs. I am simply going to expound based on my personal experiences with men. Please do not take my experiences as the be all and end all of dealing with men and their needs. I have come to my levels of wisdom based on my dealings with men, good and bad.

Here are a few psychological needs I have learned men have. If not met, they may start seeking a fantasy.

1. **The need to feel appreciated**. Men who do not feel appreciated in their existing relationship are constantly looking for the woman who will. I would venture to say this is a requirement of their current relationship.

2. **The ability to trust**. A man who cannot trust is always looking behind his back for who is out to get him, including his woman. Trust can be a beautiful thing when a man knows he can lay his head on your lap, share his deepest secrets, and not feel judged. His secrets cannot come back to haunt him in his weakest moments.

3. **The words used to address him**. Words have way more mental power than we as women will ever realize. I am sure most women are not aware of the power of their words. The power of our words can make or break a man's mental capacity. A woman must know how to speak life into a man, igniting his life and his destiny.

4. **The management of his past**. A man who has an illicit past needs a woman who knows how to handle it. She has to know how to help him navigate through the effects of his past, especially if it is damaging to his future. This must be done with care and without judgement.

5. **The state of his self-esteem**. A man with low to no self-esteem needs a woman who can build without telling him that she is building, this is why he seeks a woman. Women have the ability to nurture a man because of the motherly instinct within us. You must be wise as a serpent, know what he needs, and be willing to feed it to him on a spoon filled with honey.

We have only reviewed five aspects of what boosts or helps a man psychologically. I am sure there is so much more to this pie, but for the sake of just hitting a few points, I am going to keep it short. The question truly becomes what percentages of the whole pie does each portion make? This is a question I will have to ask in a case study for men, at a later date, lol.

I wanted to build a portion of a man's psyche, so you understand why he ventures out looking for a fantasy. When a man is not being fulfilled at home in

47

at least these areas, he seeks out the woman who will do it.

She may be the mistress. She may be his, "friend." She may be the terminology I have heard, "Work wife." Yes, there are men who work with women whom they consider their wife at work, when they have a wife at home. She may even be a family member who is unnaturally filling this void.

You see, this is a void that they desire to have filled and most men really do not care who fills it. For some men, it could mean life or death. Life or death in the sense of when their psychological needs are not being met, they can crumble and break.

The problem with this is you have some women who desire to be fulfilling this need for a man, but subconsciously, do not realize they have the need to do so. The next thing you know, this woman is taking on this role, and no commitment has been made, but yet they are feeding their own desires to be wanted, appreciated, and celebrated.

I say all this to say that for most men, I had become their fantasy. I was their fantasy because I had the ability to fill their psychological voids, and I was the mental image they had cooked up in their mind:

- ✓ Beautiful.
- ✓ A great cook.
- ✓ A prayer warrior.
- ✓ Sensitive to his personal needs.
- ✓ Able to speak life into his dead areas.
- ✓ Able to help him build his future.
- ✓ Non-judgmental about his past.
- ✓ Able to pique his destiny, helping him navigate his course.

All this, and then some!

The problem is the man whose fantasy I was, was not the man God ordained for me to be his, 'wife.' This man either did one of two things: Looked at my picture and decided to pursue me, OR he heard me speak, pray or prophesy and decided to pursue me based on the 'gifts' I possess. I have learned through so much pain and turmoil that the *gifts* I bring to the table are not the *woman* who comes to the table. Most men wanted the fantasy, but they did not want Audrea the ***woman***.

HUGE difference!

No matter where the ball fell on the court, it was all wrong. A fantasy can never become your reality when you are not prepared for the *reality* that comes with the fantasy. This was the problem my ex ran into when we began to live together. He had this fantasy of what it would be like to live with a, 'woman of God,' or a, 'preacher.'

He had no idea that living with *this* woman of God meant a truly holy lifestyle. This meant that we do not say one thing in the pulpit and then come down and live some other way. This was the behavior he was accustomed to with other ministers, and assumed *all* of us were that way.

This was not the life I had been building for 10+ years when he and I connected. I had been working hard to live a life that was pleasing before God, and I did not plan for someone to enter my life to shift the lifestyle that had me blessed up until that point. No sir, and not on any day would I live a hypocritical life.

It did not take long for him to realize that the prayer warrior whom he had befriended some years prior was on a mission to please God. He came to the realization that if he was not on the same mission, he needed to get off the train.

He had cooked up a fantasy about what he wanted to get out of me and our relationship, and guess what? Everything I mentioned in those five psyche points, He got all of the above. But what he did *not* bargain for was his need to change his lifestyle and walk into his destiny. That meant he had to truly depart from his wicked ways, get delivered and healed from the spirit of abandonment and all of its fruit. He was *not* ready for that.

The reality of living with a woman like me is the anointing on my life is real. It calls for real, permanent change and no play time with God. No one can come around me for long and remain the way they are. They will either desire change, and not know why, or they will start changing and rearranging their life because they know and understand the value of doing something different.

The problem with this is that everyone does not want to pay the price for the freedom they truly seek. It is a great conversation; it is enlightening, and invigorating. But when the proof needs to be in the pudding, most jump ship on the process necessary to create and maintain a stable life.

Such is the case with my ex-husband. I am sure he truly wanted and desired change. But when it came time to do the work, we entered a realm of no return. He was not ready to cast out the ancient spirits which came into his life while he was in the womb and most likely were built into his DNA. This is not about bashing him, but making this relationship the *reality* that I was not the fantasy he measured in his mind.

What he did *not* bargain for is the reality that behind all of that anointing and grace was a woman who was broken and hurting with low self-esteem. He did *not* bargain for the fact that he could not come to *this* table and not be able to effectively minister to my needs as a woman in that season of my life. He did *not* bargain for the fact that his perception of me was off, in the sense of me desiring to be a woman willing to financially take care of him when he had no plan or direction for life.

What he did *not* bargain for was that he would be expected to gain employment to help with bills around the house. What he did *not* bargain for is that the euphoria-based sex cloud would lift sooner than later. What h e did *not* bargain for is that the bedroom would not continue to cloud my sense of judgement. And lastly, what he did *not* bargain for was the fact that he really would be called on the carpet to create change in his life.

With all his efforts, and what he truly had *not* bargained for was that I would end the marriage. I was not going to continue carrying on with this fantasy that he had cooked up for himself and presented to me. Even milk has an expiration date, and so did his lies and fantasies.

I could probably go on and on about the woman verses the fantasy, but I am sure you get my drift, right? I was more of his fantasy than his reality. I was lightweight courted, asked to be married (with no engagement ring) and later entered into a covenant which was based on lies and a fantasy. He placed no value on the jewel I truly was and neither did I because I allowed him to get away with it. His *perception* of who I was versus who I truly was did not click until he got under the same roof with me.

Just like him, most men have this fantasy cooked up in their minds but are not prepared with the reality that comes with doing the work necessary to have a fruitful and prosperous relationship with their woman. This is why most men venture out. They venture out because they have a psychological image (fantasy) of what their woman should look like, and act like, but they have not counted the cost of what it takes to make the relationship to work. This is why fantasy is more enticing than reality.

You must also remember that the fantasy has become a world where these men mentally travel to on a regular basis. It becomes so real that they seek out the woman who fits into this world they have *created*. This is why my ex married so many times because he kept choosing the woman who was his fantasy: a fabulous woman of God. He failed on every occasion. Not because he *desired* to fail, but because he did not want to do the work associated with his fantasy. This fantasy he desired was not a bad one, it just would never become his reality because he did not want to do the work.

Ladies Watch Out…

The word of wisdom I will leave with you here is to make sure that you test him out on every side and understand his expectations from your relationship.

Not only should you understand *his* expectations, but you should also know, breathe, and understand your expectations also. You cannot go in with one desire, and then when it goes unmet, you become heartbroken when you never expressed your desires in the first place.

The flip side to all of this is that you also need to ensure you understand your assignment to that man when the relationship develops. Do not get caught into the trap that *every* man you meet is your husband. This is a trap I fell into because I was not aware of what God designed as my need from a man, verses what *I* desired to get from a man.

Huge **difference.**

I also had to identify what type of man would fit my future, and not just my present or my past. The men I was choosing were based on my past, and truthfully, my own fantasies.

If you recall, I mentioned that I once believed I was supposed to be a with a man, establishing churches and doing 'traditional' ministry. I now understand the totality of my destiny where it was not clear before.

When God called me to preach, He never intended for me to be confined to the four walls of the church. He allowed me to grow and be nurtured there, but ultimately, my destiny leads me into unconventional pathways. My anointing is diverse and I am designed to reach people in places where church won't locate them. This has *always* been my destiny. I see my vision and life's picture clearer now.

It took the wrong relationships to make this clear. Now I understand that the man designed to go with me is going with me into unconventional places and he will be comfortable there.

Will he be what the Bible declares as, "unequally yoked?" I am sure he will be, because this is my assignment as a wife. I have run from this for some time. But the most important lesson my ex-husband taught me is the power I possess as a woman to usher a man into his destiny. Not to be his crutch, but to be the one to show him his destiny through God's spiritual lens.

A woman possesses this kind of power.

The question is, will she operate in her power, or be plagued by the Red Flags? Red Flags come to bring a check to your spirit causing you to pray. Not just pray, but learn a skillful way to address it so that you are not just heard, but you evoke a man to change.

This is where the true power of a woman lies. In her authority to evoke change in that man's life.

Ladies let's be the change agent.

CHAPTER 4:

ONLINE DATING

I took the time to Google online dating, and here is what I found from Wikipedia:

Online dating (or **Internet dating**) is a system that enables people to find and introduce themselves to potential connections over the Internet, usually with the goal of developing personal, romantic, or sexual relationships.

Allow me to first start off by saying that I absolutely do *not* like online dating websites. Now, this is solely based on my experiences. It did not yield any profitable relationships, or should I obviously say that those relationships did not lead to marriage. I would say this because I had to spend so much time fishing through the fools to find the jewels. And guess what? My search came up straight empty.

AUDREA V. HEARD

There was *one* guy I dated on a regular basis but he was the mistake I made with *most* of the men I date: jumping in too fast with the marriage conviction. Now, I am sure most say that this is a conversation worth having from the beginning so that you know where both parties stand regarding marriage. But the issue I had was making him my, 'husband' way too soon into our conversations. Or becoming exclusive way too early to determine if we are compatible for each other's futures. There are always those great 'current ideas,' but do we have our future totally mapped out prior to bringing someone onto our train?

I say this because if we do not have our future mapped out for the next 5-10 years, then we really do not know if this person is a match or not. If I married the men that I *assumed* was my husband, it would have been totally disastrous when I came to the revelation of where God was taking me, futuristically. To be a world traveler, I need someone who is willing to travel the world and not be confined to the four corners of their city. If you are not matching yourself with someone who you can see in your future, then keep scrolling.

For the bulk of this chapter, I would like to talk about some do's and don'ts as it pertains to online dating. This is whether you visit a dating site, or meet someone over social media. There are some serious lines that can be crossed when we do not consider the right that can go wrong very quickly.

Here are the do's of when you meet a man online:

- ✓ *Perform a background check.* I would venture to say this is not necessary when you meet through a mutual friend, but that does not necessarily make this person solid. We do not look into their background to judge their past, but more so to know who and what you are dealing with. We cannot turn a blind eye to someone's past, these could be the Red Flags to heed or avoid.

- ✓ *Identify their friends and family.* This is very important because it can give you a side eye view of this person and what they are all about. Remember that when you are dating someone, most times they only show their best side. How friends and family respond to this person shows you what you are *really* working with.

- ✓ *Meet them over a video chat.* Someone who refuses to meet you over video chat: walk cautiously. If this person will not allow you to see them, they just may not be who they really say that they are. This is even more true when dealing with international love affairs. I won't get into it all, but I will say enough to say that men from other countries can pose as someone else, especially well-known celebrities.

59

- ✓ *Meet them in a public place for the first date.* Make sure that your first date is a public place where you won't be put in an uncomfortable position. A public place is neutral and does not put you on his territory or yours, and you are not obligated to any more than what is shared over coffee of lunch.

- ✓ *Be clear on who will pay for the first date.* I am going to step out on a limb here, but I do not mind doing so. Ladies, when you attend that first date, be prepared to go Dutch. For those who are not aware of what Dutch is, this is when both parties on a date pay for their own meal. I am suggesting this because if you meet someone on a dating site, and they foot the bill, they are more than likely in expectation of something more later, if you are following me. Not all men are this way, but most men on these dating sites are. They come prepared to pay because they want a pay back in the end.

- ✓ *Be careful how much personal information you share.* Only you can determine how much information is too much. I would venture mostly to say that there are parts of your heart that you should share in phases when this person has proven that they can be trusted. Trust is the factor of how much of yourself can be revealed and when.

✓ ***Share this relationship with someone you trust.*** I would say this is likened to the buddy system. If you are going to go out with this person, you should let someone know where you are and who you are with. This is for accountability and so that if something comes up, someone at least knows who you are with. This may mean sharing their photo with someone so that this person can be identified if necessary.

Here are the don'ts.

✓ ***Do not tell this person where you live.*** This is a major don't because you are not truly aware of who this person is. You may be inviting the midnight stalker to your home. After certain boundaries of trust have been established, then you can welcome this person to your home.

✓ ***Do not allow this person to know where you work.*** I would venture to say that for at least the first 90 days, a man should not know where you work or how much money you make. Especially if you have not verified his place of employment or occupation. I would venture to say that the majority of the time, men on dating sites are looking for women who have a means to support them. Not ALL, but *some.*

61

✓ ***Do not entertain conversations about sex.*** Most men on these sites are looking for one-night stands or women who will be easy to sleep with, especially on the first date. MOST men venture to these sites for this very reason. I met a man on one of these sites, and he flat out asked. Now mind you, he was very well aware that I was a minister, but I guess this did not mean anything to him. He *still* asked, and I politely told him no. He said that most people hooked up on these sites just for the purpose of having sex. He even continued to ask me out to an overnight stay where he contended, we could sleep in separate beds. Really? I was not surprised, but immediately came to terms in my spirit that this was not the route for me to go. And he is not the only one who came at me with this insinuation.

Unfortunately, I do not have an online dating horror story, lol. But I have had enough experience to give you some quick do's and don'ts so that you can make wise choices if you desire to go this route.

I have heard some really great love stories that have developed online and I do not doubt that God can use the internet to connect me to my true husband. But my hope on meeting my true love is in God, and not in online dating, lol.

"Red flags are moments of hesitation that determine our destination."

— *Mandy Hale*

CHAPTER 5:

THE NEGATIVE SIGNS

Red Flags. What do they *really* mean?

We've heard this term many times before, and when *you* hear this, what does it mean to *you?*

I ask the question because it was not until *after* my marriage was over that I became aware of what Red Flags were. This is probably because I was floating too long in euphoria and had not spent enough time doing what I advise be done in this book to acknowledge them.

So, what is a Red Flag? *It is used as a warning of danger.*

Before I get into the Red Flags that I desire to address, I want to deal with the warning part of a Red

Flag. I want to deal with this first because a warning is simply just that, "a warning." This means that there is something that needs to be addressed and handled in the proper manner.

When I first started out to write this book, it appeared to me that this book would remain on a negative tone. Meaning, that I would warn women of Red Flags, tell them to leave the relationship and not address them.

This is the easy way out. But what if a Red Flag comes so that you can address it? Perhaps bring it to his attention, and he uses it as an opportunity to grow within himself?

Interesting thought process, right? Yes.

This book had to be delayed in completion because it was not until recently that the Lord gave me this revelation. A Red Flag is intended to warn you so that you can bring it to this man's attention, he changes, and now the relationship can prosper. If he is *not* willing to change, then yes, pack your bags and get to stepping because that surely means there is danger ahead.

The current relationship I am in (Yes, I am seeing someone ☺), I began seeing Red Flags about this person. Not Red Flags that would break the relationship, but warnings of danger that needed to be addressed. Because of my history of throwing in the towel due to these Red Flags, it seemed like this was the logical thing to do, because this was my pattern of behavior.

I did not have a habit of addressing these issues to see if they could be resolved, I just jumped ship because it was the easiest thing to do. But in this relationship, the Lord began to deal with me about my assignment as a wife and that chances were that I would continue seeing these, 'warnings of danger' ahead, but I would have to confront them because this is what I am *assigned* as a wife to handle.

I even began to have conversation with a friend because they had been in a similar relationship. They had to break the relationship off because the Red Flags were not resolved. It was not because the Red Flags did not get addressed, but because this person refused to deal with their issues and change their ways.

I bring this up because in my personal situation, I addressed these Red Flags, and he made a shift in his behavior and way of thinking. We both had issues that we brought to our table, but we made a choice to deal with them and not run from them. This is when Red Flags become all bad. When we do not *deal* with

67

them but hide our head in the sand as if the issue does not exist.

How many relationships could possibly be spared if the Red Flags and their underlying behaviors were dealt with? Anyone who has an issue, it can be resolved, sometimes it's the way we handle it.

I wanted to address this first before I go over the Red Flags that I identify with to show you that he is *not* the one. Keep in mind that these are *my* Red Flags, and may not necessarily be yours. I say this because of what I previously said.

Red Flags *can* be dealt with. A man *can* truly come to a place of healing and restoration in his life by the pleas and prayers of the woman who is designed to bring change to his life.

Please, oh please do not read these Red Flags and take them as a ticket to dump your relationship down the gutter because a man is exhibiting these signs. I was that woman who *always* wanted to throw a man away when he did not dance to my tune. Possibly he could hear my music if I delivered it in a sweeter tone?

I am not a male relationship basher, because I believe that most women have to mature into realizing their space in a man's life. I am *that* woman. But these Red Flags also taught me that a man who does not desire to change, probably never will. This is how we will use these Red Flags to govern our relationships moving forward.

Here are our Relationship Red Flags:

1. ***He has no interest in you as a woman.*** This is a major relationship Red Flag when a man does not show interest in you and the things that make you tick. If he does not know your birthday, your favorite colors or your favorite food, then the relationship is destined to go sour at some point. This is because he is in a relationship with *you*, and not just himself. No interest expressed in you is a warning sign that you have a narcissist on your hands.

2. ***He asks you for money way too soon.*** I am in no means here to say that we should not support a man financially, because in a marriage, this very well may be the case. But a man who comes off as needy in the first 30 days, this is a major Red Flag. Now, can this be addressed? Absolutely. Give him space to explain and express himself, and then make a decision, based on the warning sign if you desire to move forward. Please know that this

is a choice, ladies. But, do not move forward with this man without some sort of solid plan of how you will handle your financial future with him.

3. *He is a trigger of traumatic events in your life.* Let's start by saying that when traumatic events are triggered, this is a cause for healing in a specific area for you. This means that you have some work to do, and you need to do it fast if you desire to remain in this relationship. I am not in any means saying that you should not continue forward, but please be mindful of what trauma is triggered. If it takes you to a place of no return, then get out *fast!* I experienced a trigger, but I realized it was **God** who allowed the trigger, and I had to get healed from the issue that was still plaguing me. Now, if your trigger is emotional or physical abuse, chances are very strong that you need to get out of that relationship quick! If not, use it as an opportunity for personal growth.

4. *He seeks personal gain from your relationship.* Please know that some men enter into certain relationships with women because they are opportunists. This is a man who sees a woman who is well off, doing her

thing and he knows exactly how to ride her curtails in order to get *himself* to the top. This is a major Red Flag because as soon as he gets where he is going, every love impression he made on you flies out the window because he has, "arrived.' The bizarre thing is that with some men, it takes a while before they exit stage left. They will stick it out for ten, twenty years or more until the whole mask is peeled off of their face. Their initial agenda has been met, and they have no more need of you. If you are a successful woman, be careful of hooking up with a man who is not on your level. Make sure you are aware of his motives and intentions, and most of all, prove his heart.

5. ***He does not respect what you have built.*** This has got to be a major issue for me as it pertains to my ex-husband. There was so much disrespect for my personal possessions, I could probably go on and on about this. The main point that I will make is that he did not respect my home possessions. He did not respect my integrity. He did not care that I had never been to jail, it was no big deal. And he could care less that my car was repossessed, everyone had lost a car in life, right? No, not me sir. Until I started dealing

71

with you, I had *never* been to jail and I had *never* had my car repossessed. Not to mention that I do not recall *ever* paying my rent or other bills late. He had no respect for what I had built because he had never taken the time to build anything himself. A man who could care less and disrespects what you have is a Red Flag that should send him packing ladies. I am not sure if there is recovery from this sort of behavior, but if there is, it can only be proven over time.

I want you to take an honest look at these five Red Flags and make the decision to leave him or work with him. I am not here to tell you what to do either way. I just want you to hear the warning signs and make your choice with a clear and stable mind. Because I did not have a stable mind some years ago, I ended up with heartache, no bank account and an empty house where the furniture my mother and I had worked so hard to achieve was stolen.

Most of the books I write are to help someone else. This experience was meant to help me first, but secondly a woman who is floating in euphoria missing the signs that this person has no desire for change, they came to use you up for all you have.

I now have a sober mind and have learned the difference. I am now aware when I am being used, verses truly being loved. *And* I have learned to identify the type of love that is being displayed towards me.

Watch out for the Red Flags ladies, but make sure you know what to do with them when they arise. You may be the woman to bring healing to a hurting heart, which is what is at the root of these behaviors. But if you cannot assist in their healing, then you are setting yourself up for the damage that brings to your life.

Make your choice. You have the power!

"When you want to fall in love, you ignore red flags in the optimistic hope."

— Max Joseph

CHAPTER 6:

EMBRACE A NEW DAY!

August 24, 2014, my divorce became final.

Wheewww!! What a relief. I was *finally* able to pick up the pieces of my life and move on. But move on to what?

Ignoring those Red Flags actually stole a total of seven years from my life. Saying, "I do" way too soon proved to be a detrimental choice that took me some time to recover from. It was a long recovery process, but I did not truly experience TOTAL recovery until 2021.

Marriage in 2010, Recovery in 2021, you do the math.

Although my ex ran off with my whole house full of

furniture, I truly realized that it was just, "stuff," and through God, I could recover all. God is such a merciful God that He allows the experiences we go through, good or bad to work out for our good. *(Romans 8:28)*

But I would be a fool to have gone through that experience and not learned *something,* right?

What is the main thing *not* to ignore? The **RED FLAGS**!!

I learned to heed the *warnings* of danger ahead and I am now equipped to take those Red Flags and do something with them. Should I have stayed and prayed for my ex-husband through his issues?

Maybe so.

But as I look back in hindsight, I am sure that my prayers would have continued to bounce off the ceiling and hit the floor because ultimately, I was not destined to be his wife. This means that my prayers would not have been life changing, sustaining prayers on his behalf.

Although he exhibited these Red Flags, I *still* learned a lot about myself as a woman. Most of all, I believe that he was a *sign* of the type of man I am assigned to marry in some aspects of the flaws he brought to the table. As a woman of God, my *first* ministry is to my husband, and I am not going to miss my God ordained assignment by attempting to save the world *first*. This is what we strong, single, saved women miss. This is a mindset of maturity, and sometimes we can only adapt it over time, and not all in one setting.

There is so much more that can be said, but the most important thing I desire you to do is embrace your **new day**. Embrace the lessons you have learned, and the wisdom nuggets I have dropped here based on my experiences.

You cannot allow your failures to take you out and lose hope on the relationship God has truly designed for you. This is what I had done. I allowed the hurt and failure of my previous marriage to feed me a lie that I would never get married again or be good enough to be loved unconditionally by another human being in the form of my husband.

But I serve notice on the enemy of my soul today that I am open to love and receive the love that God has for my life. I have proven myself in my wait, and I am ready to work on the relationship/marriage that God reserved for me. I will not throw in the towel, and I will humble myself so that I do not have to spend the rest of my days alone for fear of being hurt again. There is a man who is designed to love me as Christ loves the church, and he has been designed to help me reach certain points to my destiny. I leave my heart open and ready to love and be loved.

This is my new day, and I embrace it to the fullest. Nothing and no one will hinder who and what I am destined to have, become and be for my future husband.

How will you embrace your new day?

ABOUT THE AUTHOR

AUDREA V. HEARD

Is the CEO of Power To Wealth Enterprises, Inc., Inspired By God (IBG) Publications, Inc., Scribby Fun, Inc. & Audrea V. Heard Enterprises, LLC.

Audrea answered the call on her life to preach the Gospel of Jesus Christ in 1998 and has been on FIRE for the Lord ever since. She is anointed by God to set people free from grief and depression, stemming from the loss of a loved one.

She is a serial author and has written 17+ books to her credit. She is a full-time minister and business owner.

AUDREA V. HEARD

Other Books By The Author

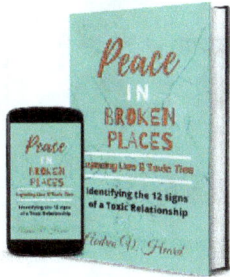

PEACE IN BROKEN PLACES

Exposing Lies & Toxic Ties

12 Signs Of A Toxic Relationship

Peace In Broken Places is a solid look at the relationships that develop in our lives when we experience times of weakness and brokenness. Discover the 12 signs of toxic relationships and how to break free from those ties! A must read for those who want to experience freedom in their life through relationships.

Available at
amazon.com

AUDREA V. HEARD

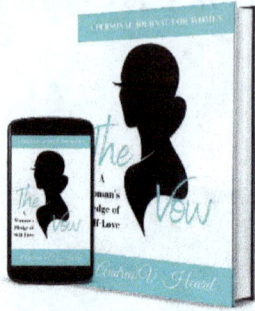

THE VOW

A WOMAN'S PLEDGE OF SELF-LOVE

The Vow was crafted in the personal prayer time of Audrea V. Heard. As she journaled, she realized she needed to take control of not just her relationships, but other areas of her life. It was after sharing her vows with a friend that she decided to make these vows public. "The Vow" promises to be a journey that will cause you to look at your life from a different perspective, causing others to see you as you see yourself.

Available at
amazon.com

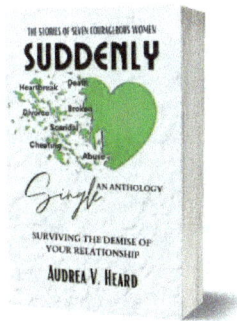

SUDDENLY SINGLE

SURVIVING THE DEMISE OF YOUR RELATIONSHIP

Courage. This is what it takes to pick up the pieces of a shattered heart. Although challenging, these women took a fearless leap and answered the call. It was a call to healing, restoration, and trust in God.

Walk with us beyond the echoes of a shattered heart onto the path of healing and redemption.

Available at
amazon.com

AUDREA V. HEARD

84

CONTACT THE AUTHOR

You can find Audrea online by visiting her website:

WWW.AudreaVHeard.Com

To book Audrea for your next event:

✉ **info@audreavheard.com**

You can follow Audrea on social media:

@AuthorAudreaHeard

AUDREA V. HEARD

www.ingramcontent.com/pod-product-compliance
Lightning Source LLC
LaVergne TN
LVHW021122080426
835513LV00011B/1205